By Paul Tillich

ON THE BOUNDARY

THE ETERNAL NOW

THE NEW BEING

THE SHAKING
OF THE FOUNDATIONS

On the Boundary

On the Boundary

AN AUTOBIOGRAPHICAL SKETCH

Paul Tillich

CHARLES SCRIBNER'S SONS, NEW YORK

TO MY WIFE

CONTENTS

On the Boundary

IN THE INTRODUCTION to my *Religiöse Verwirkli-chung* (Religious Realization) [1], I wrote: "The bound-ary is the best place for acquiring knowledge." When I was asked to give an account of the way my ideas have developed from my life, I thought that the con-cept of the boundary might be the fitting symbol for the whole of my personal and intellectual develop-ment. At almost every point, I have had to stand be-tween alternative possibilities of existence, to be com-pletely at home in neither and to take no definitive stand against either. Since thinking presupposes recep-tiveness to new possibilities, this position is fruitful for thought; but it is difficult and dangerous in life, which again and again demands decisions and thus the exclu-sion of alternatives. This disposition and its tension have determined both my destiny and my work.

BETWEEN
TWO TEMPERAMENTS

IN THE SHAPING of a child's character, one should not ascribe too much importance to the characters of its parents. There are, however, parental and ancestral traits that do recur rather strikingly in children and later descendants, and perhaps cause deep conflicts in them. Whether this is more a matter of heredity or of the impressions of early childhood is an open question. Nevertheless, I have never doubted that the union of a father from Brandenburg and a mother from the Rhineland implanted in me the tension between eastern and western Germany. In eastern Germany, an inclination to meditation tinged with melancholy, a heightened consciousness of duty and personal sin, and a strong regard for authority and feudal traditions are still alive. Western Germany is characterized by a zest for life, love of the concrete, mobility, rationality and democracy. Though neither set of characteristics was the exclusive property of either parent, it was through my parents that these conflicting traits influenced the course of my inner and outer life. The importance of such parental legacies is not that they determine the course of one's life, but that they define the scope and supply the substance out of which critical decisions are drawn.

Without this double inheritance my position on the boundary would be hard to understand. My father's influence was dominant, in part because of the early death of my mother. Consequently the character of

my mother's world asserted itself only through constant and deep struggle with that of my father. In
order for the maternal side of my makeup to express
itself, outbreaks, often extreme, were necessary. Classical composure and harmony were not part of my
heritage. This may explain why Goethe's classical
traits were alien to me, and why the pre- and post-
classical periods of Greek antiquity were more assimil-
able than the classical. This tension also accounts in
part for certain premises underlying my interpretation
of history: the choice of the line moving forward and
towards a goal rather than the classical premise of the
self-enclosed circle; the idea that the struggle between
two opposing principles constitutes the content of history; the theory of dynamic truth, which holds that
truth is found in the midst of struggle and destiny,
and not, as Plato taught, in an unchanging "beyond."

BETWEEN
CITY AND COUNTRY

BETWEEN THE AGES of four and fourteen I lived in a
small town near the Elbe, where my father was the

leading minister and the superintendent of the church district. In the small towns of many parts of Germany, the typical resident is the "farmer-burgher"—a townsman, usually well-to-do, who manages a fairly good-sized farm from his town residence. Towns of this kind have a decidedly rustic character. Many of the houses have yards, barns, and gardens attached to them, and it is only a few minutes' walk out into the fields. Cattle and sheep are herded through the streets morning and evening. Nevertheless, these are real towns with civic rights and traditions as old as the Middle Ages. The gates of the town wall open on to narrow streets with serried rows of houses and shops. The sheltered, protective quality of the town with its hustle and bustle, in contrast to the eeriness of the forest at night and the silent fields and sleepy hamlets, is one of the earliest and strongest of my childhood impressions. Visits to Berlin, where the railroad itself struck me as something half-mythical, heightened these memories and developed in me an often overpowering longing for the big city. This affected me later in many ways; it came to philosophical expression in the essays "Logos und Mythos der Technik" [2] and "Die technische Stadt als Symbol" (The Technical City as Symbol) [3].

This attraction to the city saved me from a romantic rejection of technical civilization and taught me to appreciate the importance of the city for the development of the critical side of intellectual and artistic life. Later on, I arrived at a vital and sympathetic understanding of Bohemianism, a movement that is possible only in large cities. I also learned to appreciate esthetically both the fantastic inner activity and the physical size of a city. Finally, I acquired firsthand knowledge of the political and social movements concentrated in a large city. These experiences and their lasting effect on me—the myth of the city, so to speak—are largely responsible for the popularity of my book *The Religious Situation.*[4]

My ties to the country, however, are even stronger. Nearly all the great memories and longings of my life are interwoven with landscapes, soil, weather, the fields of grain and the smell of the potato plant in autumn, the shapes of clouds, and with wind, flowers and woods. In all my later travels through Germany and southern and western Europe, the impression of the land remained strong. Schelling's philosophy of nature, which I read enthusiastically while surrounded by the beauty of nature, became the direct expression of my feeling for nature.

The weeks and, later, months that I spent by the sea every year from the time I was eight were even more important for my life and work. The experience of the infinite bordering on the finite suited my inclination toward the boundary situation and supplied my imagination with a symbol that gave substance to my emotions and creativity to my thought. Without this experience it is likely that my theory of the human boundary situation, as expressed in *Religiöse Verwicklichung*, might not have developed as it did.

There is another element to be found in the contemplation of the sea: its dynamic assault on the serene firmness of the land and the ecstasy of its gales and waves. My theory of the "dynamic mass" in the essay "Masse und Geist" (Mass and Spirit)[5], was conceived under the immediate influence of the turbulent sea. The sea also supplied the imaginative element necessary for the doctrines of the Absolute as both ground and abyss of dynamic truth, and of the substance of religion as the thrust of the eternal into finitude. Nietzsche said that no idea could be true unless it was thought in the open air. Many of my ideas were conceived in the open and much of my writing done among trees or by the sea. Alternating regularly between the elements of town and country always has been and still is part of what I consider indispensable and inviolable in my life.

BETWEEN
SOCIAL CLASSES

THE PARTICULAR NATURE of small-town life made the boundary between social classes visible to me at an early age. I attended public school, made my friends in it, and shared their animosity toward the upper class represented by my parents and the families of the mayor, the doctor, the druggist, some merchants, and a few others. Although I took private lessons in Latin with some of the children of this select group, and later on attended the *Gymnasium* in a nearby city with them, my real friends were the boys of the public school. This led to a great deal of tension with the children of my own social level, and we remained strangers throughout our schooldays. Belonging to the privileged class, therefore, aroused in me very

19

early the consciousness of social guilt that later became very important in my life and work. There seem to be only two possible outcomes when a sensitive upper-class child has an early and intimate encounter with children of the lower classes: one is the development of a consciousness of social guilt; the other—a response to the lower-class children's aggressive resentment—is class hatred. I have met both types frequently.

But my situation on the boundary with regard to social issues extends further. My father's church district included many people from the old landed nobility. Because these people were church patrons, my parents had professional and social contact with them. I was proud that I could visit their manor houses and play with their children. A descendant of one of these families, a man of rare intellectual ability, has been my lifelong friend. As a result of this borderline situation, my later opposition to the bourgeoisie (my own social class) did not itself become bourgeois, as so often happened in socialism. Instead I attempted to incorporate into socialism those elements of the feudal tradition that have an inward affinity with the socialist principle. The particular outline of religious socialism that I attempted to develop first in "Grundlinien des religiösen Sozialismus" (Principles of Religious Socialism) [6] and later in my book *Die sozialistische Entscheidung* (Socialistic Decision) [7] is rooted in this attitude. Hence it was with difficulty, and only because of the political situation of the time, that I was able to bring myself to join a party that had become as bourgeois as the Social Democrats in Germany. The essay "Das Problem der Macht: Versuch einer philosophischen Grundlegung" [8], which concerns these experiences of my youth, has been misunderstood even by some of my friends because their bourgeois pacifism lacks this particular boundary situation.

I should say something here about the civil service which, in Germany more than anywhere else, forms a separate group with its own peculiar traditions. In the narrowest sense I belong to it, both as the son of a minister who was also a school functionary and as a former professor at a Prussian university. What Prussian bureaucracy means is most clearly expressed in Kant's *Critique of Practical Reason*. It holds the primacy of the idea of duty above everything else, the valuation of law and order as the highest norm, the tendency to centralize the power of the state, a subjection to military and civil authorities, and a conscious subordination of the individual to the "organic whole." It is quite justifiable to ascribe to this very ideology the preference of much German philosophy for highly developed systems in philosophical theory and political practice. This Prussian ideology is reflected in my own life and work in several places: in my *Entwurf eines Systems der Wissenschaften* (Outline of a System of the Sciences),[9] in my readiness to subordinate myself to military and civil authorities during peace and war, and finally in my support of a political party whose program I largely opposed. To be sure, I am conscious of the limitations of this attitude. These include the tremendous burden upon my conscience, which accompanies every personal decision and every violation of tradition, an indecisiveness in the face of the new and unexpected, and a desire for an all-embracing order that would reduce the risk of personal choice.

The deep-seated aversion I felt against a distinctly bourgeois life was expressed in my preference for the small social group called "Bohemia." Artists, actors, journalists and writers were very influential within this group, which combined intellectual ferment with a genuinely non-bourgeois outlook. As a theologian and academician, I was once more on the boundary. The hallmarks of this group were an obvious lack of certain bourgeois conventions in thought and behavior, an intellectual radicalism, and a remarkable capacity for ironical self-criticism. The bohemians met at cafes, ateliers and resorts not frequented by the middle class. They were inclined toward radical political criticism and felt closer to the communist workers than to members of their own class. They followed international artistic and literary movements; they were skeptical, religiously radical, and romantic; they were antimilitaristic and influenced by Nietzsche, expressionism, and psychoanalysis.

Neither the members of the feudal order nor the well-to-do bourgeois opposed the "bohemian" groups; and conversely both were always able to gain admittance in the bohemian group. In exchange for membership, they offered the bohemians social and economic privileges. Opposition came from the petit bourgeoisie, the lower middle class, with its prejudices and pretensions, its unconcern for intellectual and especially artistic problems, its need for security, and its distrust of the intelligentsia. The fact that I was never seriously involved in the life of the petit bourgeoisie but rather, like many from its ranks, repudiated it with an apparent, if only half-conscious, arrogance was to shape both my intellectual and my personal destiny. Intellectually, the struggle to overcome the narrowness of the petit bourgeoisie constantly opened up new vistas which in turn made it difficult for me to find any intellectual or social resting place. I came under personal attack from the reactionary revolution of the middle class, which hit the intelligentsia hard and finally destroyed it. The spiteful persecution of the German intelligentsia by representatives of a romantic middle-class ideology (Nazism) was in response to the intelligentsia's partially justified and partially unjustified repudiation of the middle class.

BETWEEN
REALITY AND
IMAGINATION

THE DIFFICULTIES I experienced in coming to terms with reality led me into a life of fantasy at an early age. Between fourteen and seventeen, I withdrew as often as possible into imaginary worlds which seemed to be truer than the world outside. In time, that romantic imagination was transformed into philosophical imagination. For good and for ill, the latter has stayed with me ever since. It has been good in that it has given me the ability to combine categories, to perceive abstractions in concrete terms (I would almost say "in color") and to experiment with a wide range of conceptual possibilities. It has been of doubtful value insofar as such imaginative ability runs a risk of mistaking the creations of the imagination for realities, that is, of neglecting experience and rational critique, of thinking in monologues rather than dialogues, and of isolating itself from cooperative scientific effort. Whether good or bad, this imaginative tendency (plus certain other circumstances), prevented me from becoming a scholar in the accepted sense of the word. Amongst intellectuals of the twenties there was a kind of aversion against the scholar in the restricted sense of "expert."

Imagination manifests itself, among other ways, in a delight in play. This delight has accompanied me all my life, in games, in sports (which I never took as more than play), in entertainment, in the playful emotion that accompanies productive moments and makes them expressions of the sublimest form of human freedom. The romantic theory of play, Nietzsche's preference for play as opposed to "the spirit of gravity,"

Kierkegaard's "esthetic sphere," and the imaginative element in mythology were always both attractive and dangerous to me. Perhaps it was an awareness of this danger that drove me more and more to the uncompromising seriousness of prophetic religion. My comments in *Die sozialistische Entscheidung* (Socialistic Decision) [10] about the mythological consciousness were a protest not only against the ultimate lack of seriousness in nationalistic paganism, but also against the mythical-romantic element not conquered in myself.

Art is the highest form of play and the genuinely creative realm of the imagination. Though I have not produced anything in the field of the creative arts, my love for the arts has been of great importance to my theological and philosophical work. At home my father maintained the musical traditions associated with the evangelical ministry. He himself wrote music. Like most German Protestants, however, he cared little for architecture and the fine arts. Since I am not artistically inclined and only later gained an appreciation of the visual arts, my longing for art was directed toward literature. This was in line with the humanist tradition in education at the *Gymnasium*. Schlegel's classical German translation of Shakespeare became particularly important for me. I identified myself (almost dangerously) with figures like Hamlet. My instinctive sympathy today for what is called existentialism goes back in part to an existential understanding of this great work of literature. Neither Goethe nor Dostoievsky had a similar effect on me. I came to know Dostoievsky too late in my life. Goethe's work seemed to express too little of the boundary situation in the Kierkegaardian sense; it did not then seem to be existential enough, although I have revised this judgment in my maturity. Even after my infatuation with Hamlet, which lasted for some time, I preserved the capacity for complete identification with other creatures of poetic fancy. The specific mood, the color as it were, of certain weeks or months of my life, would be determined by one literary work or the other. Later this was especially true of novels which I read infrequently but with great intensity.

Literature, however, contains too much philosophy to be able to satisfy fully the desire for pure artistic contemplation. The discovery of painting was a crucial experience for me. It happened during World War I, as a reaction to the horror, ugliness and destructiveness of war. My delight even in the poor reproductions obtainable at the military bookstores developed into a systematic study of the history of art. And out of this study came the experience of art; I recall most vividly my first encounter—almost a revelation—with a Botticelli painting in Berlin during my last furlough of the war. Out of the philosophical and theological reflection that followed these experiences, I developed some fundamental categories of philosophy of religion and culture, viz., form and substance. It was the expressionist style emerging in Germany during the first decade of this century and winning public recognition following the war and the bitter struggle with an uncomprehending lower middle-class taste that opened my eyes to how the substance of a work of art could destroy form and to the creative ecstasy implied in this process. The concept of the "breakthrough," which dominates my theory of revelation, is an example of the use of this insight.

Later, when expressionism gave way to a new realism, I developed my concept of "belief-ful realism" from a study of the new style. The idea of "belief-ful realism" is the central concept of my book, *The Religious Situation*,[11] which for that reason is dedicated to an artist friend. My impressions of various representations of individuals and groups in Western art gave me the inspiration and material for a lecture, "Masse und Persönlichkeit" (Mass and Personality).[12] My growing preference for the old Church and her solutions to such theological problems as "God and the World," "Church and State," was nourished by the deep impression made on me by early Christian art in Italy. The mosaics in the ancient Roman basilicas accomplished what no amount of studying church history could have done. My interest in painting is directly reflected in the article, "Stil und Stoff in der bildenden Kunst" (Style and Material in Plastic Art), in my address at the opening of an exhibition of religious art in Berlin in 1930, in the pertinent sections of *Das System der Wissenschaften nach Gegenständen und Methoden* (System of the Sciences),[13] in my "Religionsphilosophie" (Philosophy of Religion),[14] and in *The Religious Situation.*

This vital experience of modern painting also opened the way for an appreciation of modern German literature, as represented by Hofmannsthal, George, Rilke, and Werfel. I was most deeply impressed by the later poetry of Rilke. Its profound psychoanalytical realism, mystical richness, and a poetic form charged with metaphysical content made this poetry a vehicle for insights that I could elaborate only abstractly through the concepts of my philosophy of religion. For myself and my wife, who introduced me to poetry, these poems became a book of devotions that I read again and again.

BETWEEN
THEORY AND PRACTICE

I NEVER DOUBTED—nor did anyone else—that I was destined to a life devoted to intellectual rather than practical matters. I was about eight when I first wrestled with the idea of the Infinite. In school and in my pre-confirmation instruction, I was fascinated with Christian dogmatics; I devoured popular books on philosophy. My education in the humanistic tradition and my enthusiasm for the language and literature of the Greeks strengthened this disposition toward the theoretical. I fully agreed with Aristotle's contention, as expressed in the *Nichomachean Ethics*, that pure contemplation alone offers pure happiness. My inward struggles with the truth of traditional religion also helped keep me within the domain of the speculative. In the religious life, however, contemplation implies something other than philosophical intimations of Being. In religious truth, one's very existence is at stake. The question is: to be or not to be. Religious truth is existential truth; to this extent it cannot be separated from practice. Religious truth is *acted*, as the Gospel of John says.

It soon became clear, though, that a one-sided devotion to contemplation was based on the same escape from reality as my flight into literary fantasy. As soon as I recognized this danger and was confronted with practical tasks, I threw myself into them with complete ardor—partly to the advantage and partly to the disadvantage of my intellectual pursuits. The first example of this plunge into day-by-day affairs was my active participation in a student organization called *Wingolf*. The tensions between its Christian principles and modern liberal ideas and practices, as well as those personal tensions that readily flare up in groups of young students, gave rise to many questions of practical policy, especially during the time when I was a leader of the organization. The question of the principles of a Christian community was so thoroughly argued out in the group that all who were active in the struggle profited a great deal by it. During that time I came to understand the value of objective statements like denominational creeds. If a community gives general recognition to a confessional foundation whose meaning transcends subjective belief or doubt, it will hold together even while allowing room for tendencies toward doubt, criticism, and uncertainty.

My university studies were followed by two years of parish work and four years as a field chaplain on the Western front. After the war I spent a brief period in church administrative work. My theoretical studies were severely restricted, though not entirely interrupted, during these years of practical activity. This time of immersion in practical problems, however, did not shake my basic devotion to the theoretical life.

The tension between theory and practice was heightened at the outbreak of the revolution. For the first time, I became very much alive to the political situation. Like most German intellectuals before 1914, I had been rather indifferent to politics. Our consciousness of social guilt had not expressed itself politically. It was during the collapse of imperial Germany and the revolution of the last year of World War I that I began to understand such issues as the political background of the war, the interrelation of capitalism and imperialism, the crisis of bourgeois society, and the schisms between classes. The tremendous pressure of the war, which had threatened to obscure the idea of God or to give it demonic coloration, found an outlet in the discovery of the human responsibility for the war and the hope for a refashioning of human society. When the call to a <u>religious socialist movement</u> was sounded, I could not and would not refuse to heed it. At first we worked only on theoretical problems of "religion and socialism." The working circle to which I belonged was a group of professors, Mennicke, Heimann, Löw and others, all explicitly concerned with theory. But the goal of our work was political, and we were thus inevitably faced with problems of practical politics which often conflicted with theoretical positions. This conflict was reflected in our discussion of the influence of religious socialism on the churches, the political parties and, insofar as we were professors, the universities.

In the Evangelical Church a league of religious socialists had been formed with the aim of closing the gap between the Church and the Social Democratic Party through changes in church policy and also through theoretical discussion. Believing that its theoretical foundations were inadequate, I kept aloof from the group, perhaps unjustifiably, and thus missed an opportunity for being active in ecclesiastical politics. This time the tension between theory and practice was resolved wholly in favor of theory, though perhaps not for its benefit.

So too it was with my relations to the Social Democratic Party. I became a member in order to influence it by contributing to the elaboration of its theoretical base. For this purpose I joined with my friends of the religious-socialist group to found the magazine *Neue Blätter für den Sozialismus.*[15] Through it we hoped to revitalize the rigid theology of German socialism and to remold it from a religious and philosophical standpoint. I myself did not engage in practical politics, but since many of my co-workers were very active politically, our magazine was drawn into the problems of the existing political situation. Of course, I did not refuse specific tasks. But I did not look for them, perhaps once more to the detriment of theoretical work that was intended to serve a political end and to supply the conceptual form of a political movement. On the other hand, even those comparatively rare contacts with practical politics interrupted the concentration that my professional work so urgently required.

The tension between theory and practice came to a head in the post-war discussion about the reorganization of the German universities. In the course of the nineteenth century, the old humanistic ideal of classicism was undermined by the specialization of the sciences and by an increased demand, quantitative and qualitative, for professional training. With the heavy influx of students we could no longer even pretend to uphold the classical ideal of the "well rounded" man. Weak compromises were invented to cover up the discrepancy between the ideal and reality. In an essay published in the *Frankfurter Zeitung,* November 22, 1931, I proposed a plan for a twofold educational program that prompted a storm of approval and protest. On the one hand, I advocated the establishment of professional schools and, on the other, a liberal arts faculty that would be freed from the tasks of professional training to represent the old idea of the university. Both were to be interrelated yet different in aim and method. The liberal arts faculty was to be permeated by the spirit of that philosophy whose task is the illumination of the question of human existence by means of the Logos. There was to be radical questioning without regard for political or religious allegiances. At the same time, the educational philosophy of the faculty was to be fully informed by the spiritual and social problems of contemporary life. Any great creative philosophy must meet these demands. It was an indication of weakness when, in the nineteenth century, philosophy became, with few exceptions, more and more a tool of the schools and of the "professors of philosophy." It is, however, no less destructive of philosophy whenever our own century endeavors to suppress radical questions by political means and to dictate a political world view. The "political university" of today sacrifices theory to practice. This, like its opposite, is fatal to both types of university. At present the boundary between theory and practice has become a battlefield on which the fate of the university of the future, and with it the fate of humanist culture in a civilized world, will be decided.

BETWEEN
HETERONOMY AND
AUTONOMY

I WAS ABLE to reach intellectual and moral autonomy only after a severe struggle. My father's authority, which was both personal and intellectual and which, because of his position in the church, I identified with the religious authority of revelation, made every attempt at autonomous thinking an act of religious daring and connected criticism of authority with a sense of guilt. The age-old experience of mankind, that new knowledge can be won only by breaking a taboo and that all autonomous thinking is accompanied by a consciousness of guilt, is a fundamental experience of my own life. As a result, every theological, ethical, and political criticism encountered inner obstacles that were overcome only after lengthy struggles. This heightened for me the significance, seriousness, and weight of such insights. When I would belatedly arrive at a conclusion that had long since become commonplace to the average intelligence, it still seemed to me to be shocking and full of revolutionary implications. Free-wheeling intelligence was suspect to me. I had scant confidence in the creative power of purely autonomous thought. In this spirit I delivered a series of university lectures dealing specifically with the catastrophic failures, past and present, of autonomous thought, e.g., the development of Greek philosophy from the emergence of rational autonomy and its decline into skepticism and probabilism to the return

37

to the "new archaism" of late antiquity. It constituted for me conclusive historical evidence of the inability of autonomous reason to create by itself a world with real content. In lectures on medieval philosophy, on the intellectual history of Protestantism, and in my essay *The Religious Situation,* I applied this idea to the history of Western thought and derived from it the need for a theonomy, that is, an autonomy informed by a religious substance.

The critique of pure autonomy was not meant to ease the way to a new heteronomy. Submission to divine or secular authorities, i.e., heteronomy, was precisely what I had rejected. I neither can nor want to return to it. If the existing trend of events in Europe is moving toward a return to both old and new heteronomies, I can only protest passionately, even while I understand the motives for the trend. An autonomy won in hard struggle is not surrendered so readily as one that always has been accepted as a matter of fact. Once a man has broken with the taboos of the most sacred authorities, he cannot subject himself to another heteronomy, whether religious or political. That such submission has become so easy for so many in our day is a consequence of the emptiness and skepticism surrounding most traditional authority. Freedom that has not been fought for and for which no sacrifices have been made is easily cast aside. It is only thus that we can understand the desire for a new bondage among European youth (leaving sociological factors aside).

I have long been opposed to the most expressly ✳ heteronomous religious system, Roman Catholicism. This protest was both Protestant and autonomous. It was never directed, in spite of theological differences, against the dogmatic values or liturgical forms in the Roman Catholic system but rather against Catholicism's heteronomous character with its assertion of a dogmatic authority that is valid even when submission to it is only superficial. Only once did I with any seriousness entertain the idea of becoming a Catholic. In 1933, before the awakening of German Protestantism to the meaning of Nazism, I seemed to have only two alternatives: either the Roman church or a nationalist paganism in Protestant dress. In deciding between these two heteronomies, I would have had to choose Catholicism. I did not have to make that choice because German Protestantism remembered its Christian foundation.

The struggle between autonomy and heteronomy reappears at another level in Protestantism. It was pre-

cisely through my protest against Protestant orthodoxy, even in its moderate nineteenth-century form,
that I found my way to autonomy. For this reason,
my fundamental theological problem arose in apply-
ing the relation of the absolute, which is implied in the
idea of God, to the relativity of human religion. Religious dogmatism, including that of Protestant orthodoxy and the most recent phase of what is called
dialectical theology, comes into being when a historical religion is cloaked with the unconditional validity
of the divine, as when a book, person, community,
institution, or doctrine claims absolute authority and
demands the submission of every other reality; for no
other claim can exist beside the unconditioned claim
of the divine. But that this claim can be grounded in a
finite, historical reality is the root of all heteronomy
and all demonism. The demonic is something finite
and limited which has been invested with the stature
of the infinite. Its demonic character becomes clear as,
sooner or later, another finite reality also claiming in-
finitude opposes it so that human consciousness is
severed between the two.

Karl Barth has said that my negative attitude toward heteronomy and my use of the word demonic to
describe it represents a struggle against the Grand In-

quisitor (as portrayed in Dostoievsky's *The Brothers Karamazov*) that is no longer necessary today. I think that the development of the German Confessional Church in the last years proves how necessary the struggle remains. The Grand Inquisitor is now entering the Confessional Church wearing the strong but tight-fitting armor of Barthian supranaturalism. The extremely narrow position of the Barthians may save German Protestantism, but it also creates a new heteronomy, an anti-autonomous and anti-humanistic attitude that I must regard as a denial of the Protestant principle. For Protestantism will continue to be something more than a weakened version of Catholicism only so long as the protest against every one of its own realizations remains alive within it. This Protestant protest is not rational criticism but prophetic judgment. It is not autonomy but theonomy, even when it appears, as often happens, in rationalistic and humanistic forms. In the theonomous, prophetic word, the contradiction between autonomy and heteronomy is overcome.

But if protest and prophetic criticism are necessary elements of Protestantism, the question arises as to how Protestantism can be embodied in the world. Worship, preaching, and instruction presuppose expressions of the substance that can be handed on. The institutional church and even the prophetic word itself require a sacramental basis, an incarnate life to draw upon. Life cannot stand only on its own boundaries; it must also live at its center, out of its own abundance. The Protestant principle of criticism and protest is a necessary corrective, but is not in itself constructive. In cooperation with others, I contributed an essay to the book, *Protestantismus als Kritik und Gestaltung* (Protestantism as Criticism and Construction) [16], dealing with the question of the realization of Protestantism. The title of my first large theological work, *Religiöse Verwirklichung* (Religious Realization) [17], was prompted by this problem. Protestantism must live within the tension between the sacramental and the prophetic, between the constitutive and the corrective. If these elements were to separate, the former would become heteronomous and the latter empty. Their unity, as symbol and as reality, seems to me to be given in the New Testament picture of the crucified Christ. There the highest human religious possibility is manifested and sacrificed at the same time.

The events of the last few years in German Protestantism and the emergence of neo-paganisms on Christian soil have given new importance to the problem of religious autonomy and heteronomy. The question of the final criterion for human thought and action has become acute today as never before since the struggle between Roman paganism and early Christianity. The Nazi attack of the cross as the criterion of every human creation has renewed our understanding of the meaning of the cross. The question of heteronomy and autonomy has become the question of the final criterion of human existence. In this struggle, the destiny of German Christendom, of the German nation, and of Christian nations in general is being decided.

Every political system requires authority, not only in terms of possessing instruments of force but also in terms of the silent or express consent of the people. Such consent is possible only if the group in power stands for an idea that is powerful and significant for all. Thus, in the political sphere there is a relationship of authority and autonomy which in my essay, "Der Staat als Erwartung und Aufgabe" (The State as Promise and Task) [18] I have characterized as follows, "Every political structure presupposes power and, consequently, a group in power. Since a power group is also a cluster of interests opposed to other units of interest, it is always in need of a corrective. Democracy is justifiable and necessary insofar as it is a system that incorporates correctives against the misuse of political authority. It becomes untenable as soon as it hinders the emergence of a power group. This occurred in the Weimar Republic, whose particular democratic form made it impossible from the start for any group to gain power. On the other hand, the corrective against the abuse of authority by the power group is lacking in dictatorial systems. The result is the enslavement of the entire nation and the corruption of the ruling class." Since making my first political decision a few years before World War I, I have stood with the political left, even to opposing very strong conservative traditions. This was a protest against political heteronomy, just as my earlier protest against religious heteronomy led me to side with liberal theology. In spite of all my subsequent criticism of economic liberalism, it was and is impossible for me to join the all-too-common depreciation of "liberal thinking." I would rather be accused of being "liberalistic" than of ignoring the great, and truly human, liberal principle of autonomy.

Nevertheless, the question of political power remained urgent during a period in which one of our most difficult political problems was reintegrating the disintegrated masses of modern capitalism. I dealt with this problem in connection with recent events in German history in an essay, "The Totalitarian State and the Claims of the Church." [19] In it I stressed that an authoritarian engulfment of the masses is inevitable when they have been deprived of all meaningful existence. There are also important reflections on this problem in my book, *Masse und Geist* (Mass and Spirit) [20], which appeared soon after the war. In the chapter, "Mass and the Personality," I argued that only specialized esoteric groups should strive for an autonomous position. The retreat to an esoteric autonomy seemed to me to be demanded by the forces of history operating in the present (which are roughly comparable to those of late antiquity). Just how this retreat is to be accomplished without too great a sacrifice of truth and justice is a strategic problem for future generations. It will be both a political and religious problem. I am determined to stand on the boundary between autonomy and heteronomy, in principle and in fact. I intend to remain on this boundary even if the coming historical era should fall under the sway of heteronomy.

BETWEEN
THEOLOGY AND
PHILOSOPHY

THE BOUNDARY SITUATION from which I am trying to explain my life and thought is most clearly seen at this point. Ever since the last years of my secondary education, I wanted to be a philosopher. I used every free hour to read those philosophical books that came by chance into my hands. I found Schwegler's *Geschichte der Philosophie* (History of Philosophy) in the dusty corner of a country preacher's bookshelf, and Fichte's *Wissenschaftslehre* (Theory of Science) on top of a wagon load of books on a Berlin street. In a state of boyish excitement, I bought Kant's *Critique of Pure Reason* from a bookstore for the immense price of fifty cents. These works, especially that of Fichte, introduced me to the most difficult aspects of German philosophy. Discussions with my father, who was an examiner in philosophy on the committee which examined students for the ministry, enabled me from the beginning of my university career to carry on discussions with older students and young instructors about idealism and realism, freedom and determinism, God and the world. Fritz Medicus, who was philosophy professor at Halle and later at Zürich, was my teacher in philosophy. His work on Fichte initiated the rediscovery of Fichte's philosophy at the turn of the century that ultimately led to a general renaissance of German idealism. Partly through the accident of a bargain purchase, and partly through an inner affinity for his work, I came under the influence of Schelling. I read through his collected works several times, and eventually made his work the subject of my dissertations for the degrees of doctor of philosophy and licentiat of theology. The latter dissertation was published in book form as *Mystik und Schuldbewusstsein in Schellings philosophischer Entwicklung* (Schelling's Philosophical Development).

During this time I also studied Protestant theology, and at the conclusion of my studies I became an assistant pastor in various parishes of the "Old Prussian United Church." My most important theological teachers were Martin Kähler and Wilhelm Lütgert, both of Halle. Kähler was a man whose intellectual ability and moral and religious power were overwhelming. As a teacher and writer he was difficult to understand. In many respects he was the most profound and most modern representative of the nineteenth-century theology of mediation. He was an opponent of Albrecht Ritschl, a proponent of the theological doctrine of justification, and a critic of the idealism and humanism from which he was himself intellectually descended.

I am indebted to him primarily for the insight that he gave me into the all-embracing character of the Pauline-Lutheran idea of justification. On the one hand, the doctrine of justification denies every human claim before God and every identification of God and man. On the other hand, it declares that the estrangement of human existence, its guilt and despair, are overcome through the paradoxical judgment that before God the sinner is just. My christology and dogmatics were informed by the interpretation of Christ's crucifixion as the event in history through which the divine judgment against the world becomes concrete and manifest. Thus it was easy for me to make a connection between my theology and that of Karl Barth, and to accept the analysis of human existence given by Kierkegaard and Heidegger. However, it was difficult and even impossible for me to reconcile my thinking with liberal dogmatics, which replaces the crucified Christ with the historical Jesus and dissolves the paradox of justification into moral categories.

In spite of my negative attitude toward liberal dogmatics, I am deeply appreciative of the liberal movement's historical accomplishments. I soon parted company with the Halle theologians over this issue, and I found myself less and less in accord with the Barthian neo-supranaturalism that wishes to resurrect the dogmatic doctrines of the Reformation by bypassing the scientific work of the last two hundred years. The historical interpretation of the Old Testament developed by Wellhausen and Gunkel, the so-called *religionsgeschichtliche* method, caught my interest and helped me to understand the fundamental significance of the Old Testament for Christianity and for mankind. An enthusiasm for the Old Testament has stayed with me, and through its bearing on my political positions it has decisively shaped my life and thought.

I owe my historical insights into the New Testament principally to Schweitzer's *The Quest of the Historical Jesus* and Bultmann's *The Synoptic Tradition*. When I read the work of Ernst Troeltsch I finally shed the last remnants of my interest in the theology of mediation and its apologetics and turned to church history and the problem of historical criticism. The documentary proof of this change of interest is a set of propositions which I presented to a group of theological friends in 1911. I asked how Christian doctrine might be understood if the non-existence of the historical Jesus were to become historically probable, and then attempted to answer my own question. Even now I insist on raising this question radically rather than falling back on the kind of compromises that I encountered then and that Emil Brunner is now offering. The foundation of Christian belief is the biblical picture of Christ, not the historical Jesus. The criterion of human thought and action is the picture of Christ as it is rooted in ecclesiastical belief and human experience, not the shifting and artificial construct of historical research. Because I took this position I was called a radical theologian in Germany, whereas Americans call me a Barthian. But agreement with the Barthian paradox, the mystery of justification, does not mean agreement with Barthian supranaturalism; and agreement with the historical and critical achievement of liberal theology does not mean agreement with liberal dogmatics.

I managed to reconcile the doctrine of justification

with radical historical criticism by developing an interpretation of the idea of justification that has been of the greatest importance to me, both personally and professionally. I applied the doctrine of justification to the sphere of human thought. Not only human acts but human thinking as well stand under the divine "No." No one, not even a believer or a Church, can boast of possessing truth, just as no one can boast of possessing love. Orthodoxy is intellectual pharisaism. The justification of the doubter corresponds to the justification of the sinner. Revelation is just as paradoxical as the forgiveness of sins. Neither can become an object of possession. I developed these ideas in the essays, "Rechtfertigung und Zweifel" (Justification and Doubt) [21] and "Die Idee der Offenbarung" (The Idea of Relevation).[22]

It was the work of Schelling, particularly his late thought, which helped me relate these basic theological ideas to my philosophical development. Schelling's philosophical interpretation of Christian doctrine opened the way, I thought, to a unification of theology and philosophy. His development of a Christian philosophy of existence, as opposed to Hegel's humanistic philosophy of essence, and his interpretation of history as *Heilsgeschichte*, moved in the same direc-

51

tion. I confess that even today I find more "theonomous philosophy" in Schelling than in any of the
other German idealists. But not even he was able to
achieve a unity of theology and philosophy. World
War I was disastrous for idealistic thought in general.
Schelling's philosophy was also affected by this catas-
trophe. The chasm that he had seen but soon covered
up again opened itself anew. The experience of those
four years of war revealed to me and to my entire
generation an abyss in human existence that could not
be ignored. If a reunion of theology and philosophy is
ever to be possible it will be achieved only in a synthesis that does justice to this experience of the abyss
in our lives. My philosophy of religion has attempted
to meet this need. It consciously remains on the
boundary between theology and philosophy, taking
care not to lose the one in the other. It attempts to express the experience of the abyss in philosophical concepts and the idea of justification as the limitation of
philosophy. A lecture which I delivered before the
Kant Society of Berlin, "Die Überwindung des Religionsbegriffs in der Religionsphilosophie" (The Elimi-
nation of the Concept Religion in the Philosophy of
Religion) [23], reflects this paradoxical attempt even in its
title.

A philosophy of religion, however, is shaped by philosophical concepts as well as by religious reality. My own philosophical position developed in critical dialogue with neo-Kantianism, the philosophy of value, and phenomenology. I accepted their common rejection of positivism, especially in the psychologistic guise that it assumed in philosophy of religion. Husserl's *Logische Untersuchungen* (Studies in Logic) in which psychologism is most forcefully rejected, confirmed what I had learned from Kant and Fichte. But I could not attach myself to any of the three positions. Because of its panlogistical tendency, neo-Kantianism could not comprehend the experience of the abyss and the paradox. I could not accept the philosophy of value because it too is neo-Kantian and because its attempt to understand religion as a realm of value contradicts the transcendence of values which is assumed in the experience of the abyss. Phenomenology lacks the element of dynamism and also furthers Catholic-conservative tendencies, as can be seen from the biographies of the bulk of its proponents.

Nietzsche, whom I did not read until I was thirty, made a tremendous impression on me. Nietzschean vitalism expresses the experience of the abyss more

clearly than neo-Kantianism, value-philosophy, or
phenomenology. The ecstatic affirmation of existence
so prevalent after the war as a reaction to the wartime
years of death and hunger made Nietzsche's affirmation of life very attractive. Because it is, at least
partly, historically rooted in Schelling's thought, I
could readily accept it. I might well have developed
my philosophy along these lines, incorporating pagan
elements instead of Jewish and Catholic motifs; but
the experience of the German revolution of 1918 decisively redirected my concerns toward a sociologically
based and politically oriented philosophy of history.
My study of Troeltsch had paved the way for this
change of direction. I clearly remember the statement
he made during his first Berlin lecture on the philosophy of history, claiming that his was the first philosophical treatment of this subject at the University of
Berlin since Hegel's death. Although we were to a
great extent agreed about the problems involved, I repudiated his idealistic point of departure. Troeltsch's
idealism made it impossible for him to overcome
what he called historicism, against which he fought.
Historicism could be overcome only by a generation
that had been forced to make fundamental historical
decisions. In light of the necessity of facing history

squarely—a demand that is both grounded in and limited by the Christian paradox—I sought to develop a philosophy of history that could become also a philosophy of religious socialism.

Anyone standing on the boundary between theology and philosophy must necessarily develop a clear conception of the logical relation between them. I attempted to do this in my book *Das System der Wissenschaften* (System of the Sciences).[24] My ultimate concern there was with the questions: How can theology be a science in the sense of *Wissenschaft?* How are its several disciplines related to the other sciences? What is distinctive about its method?

I answered by classifying all of the methodological disciplines as sciences of thinking, being, and culture; by maintaining that the foundation of the whole system of sciences is the philosophy of meaning (*Sinnphilosophie*); by defining metaphysics as the attempt to express the Unconditioned in terms of rational symbols, and by defining theology as theonomous metaphysics. In this way I attempted to win a place for theology within the totality of human knowledge. The success of this analysis presupposes that the theonomous character of knowledge itself must be acknowledged; that is to say, we must understand that thought

55

itself is rooted in the Absolute as the ground and abyss of meaning. Theology takes as its explicit object that which is the implicit presupposition of all knowledge. Thus theology and philosophy, religion and knowledge, embrace one another. In light of the boundary position, this appears as their real relationship.

When existential philosophy was introduced into Germany, I came to a new understanding of the relationship between theology and philosophy. Heidegger's lectures at Marburg, the publication of his *Sein und Zeit* (Being and Time), and also his interpretation of Kant were significant in this connection. Both to the followers and to the opponents of existential philosophy, Heidegger's work is more important than anything since Husserl's *Logische Untersuchungen* (Studies in Logic). Three factors prepared the ground for my acceptance of existential philosophy. The first was my close knowledge of Schelling's final period, in which he outlined his philosophy of existence in response to Hegel's philosophy of essence. The second was my knowledge, however limited, of Kierkegaard, the real founder of existential philosophy. The final factor was my enthusiasm for Nietzsche's "philosophy of life." These three elements are also present in Heidegger. Their fusion into a kind of mysticism tinged with Augustinianism accounts for the fascination of Heidegger's philosophy. Much of its terminology is found in the sermon literature of German Pietism. His interpretation of human existence implies and develops, however unintentionally, a doctrine of man that is one of human freedom and finitude. It is so closely related to the Christian interpretation of human existence that one is forced to describe it as "Theonomous philosophy" in spite of Heidegger's emphatic atheism. To be sure, it is not a philosophy which presupposes the theological answer to the question of human finitude and then explains it in philosophical terms. That would be a variant of idealism and the opposite of a philosophy of existence. Existential philosophy asks in a new and radical way the question whose answer is given to faith in theology.

These ideas, which I developed in my Yale University lectures, led to a sharper distinction between theology and philosophy than my earlier philosophy of religion had made. But I have never denied their mutual relatedness.

My professional career has also been "on the boundary" between the two disciplines. I received the degrees of Doctor of Philosophy in Breslau and Licentiat in Theology and later Doctor of Theology (*honoris causa*) in Halle; I was Lecturer in Theology in Berlin, Professor of the Science of Religion in Dresden and Professor Honorarius of Theology in Leipzig, Professor Ordinarius of Philosophy in Frankfurt-on-Main, and Visiting Professor of Philosophical Theology at Union Theological Seminary in New York. A constant change of faculties and yet no change in subject matter! As a theologian I have tried to remain a philosopher, and vice versa. It would have been easier to abandon the boundary and to choose one or the other. Inwardly this course was impossible for me. Fortunately, outward opportunities matched my inward inclinations.

BETWEEN
CHURCH AND SOCIETY

ALTHOUGH I HAVE often criticized Church doctrine and practice, the Church has always been my home. This became very clear to me at the time when neopagan ideas were making their way into it and when I feared that I would lose my religious as well as my political home. The peril made me conscious of the fact that I belonged to the Church. This feeling grew out of the experiences of my early years—the Christian influence of a Protestant minister's home and the relatively uninterrupted religious customs of a small east-German city at the close of the nineteenth century. My love for church buildings and their mystic atmosphere, for liturgy and music and sermons, and for the great Christian festivals that molded the life of the town for days and even weeks of the year left an indelible feeling in me for the ecclesiastical and sacramental. To these must be added the mysteries of Christian doctrine and their impact on the inner life of a child, the language of the Scriptures, and the exciting experiences of holiness, guilt, and forgiveness. All this played a crucial part in my decision to become a theologian and to remain one. My ordination, my pastoral activities, the interest in sermons and liturgy that persisted long after I moved into a university environment, were all outgrowths of the realization that I belonged within the Church.

But here, too, I was on the boundary. A sense of alienation accompanied my increasing criticism of the doctrines and institutions of the Church. My contact with the intelligentsia and the proletariat outside the Church was crucial in this connection. I did not encounter the intelligentsia outside the Church until rather late, after finishing my theological studies. In this encounter my attitude was apologetic in accordance with my borderline position. To be apologetic means to defend oneself before an opponent with a common criterion in view. When apologists of the ancient church were vindicating themselves before an aggressive paganism, the commonly acknowledged criterion was the Logos—theoretical and practical reason. Because the apologists equated Christ with the Logos, and the divine commands with the rational law of nature, they could plead the cause of Christian doctrine and practice before their pagan opponents. In our day, apologetics does not mean erecting a new principle in opposition to existing intellectual and moral standpoints. Its task is to defend the Christian principle against emerging rival positions. The decisive question for both ancient and modern apologetics is that of the common criterion, the court of judgment where the dispute can be settled.

In my search for this common criterion I discovered that the modern trends of thought which are rooted in the Enlightenment are substantially Christian, in spite of their critical attitude toward ecclesiastical Christianity. They are not, as they are often called, pagan. Paganism, especially in nationalistic garb, first appeared after World War I in connection with the complete disintegration of Christian humanism. There is no such thing as apologetics in the face of this kind of paganism. The only question is survival or extinction. This is the same struggle that prophetic monotheism has always carried on against demonic polytheism. Apologetics was possible in antiquity only because polytheism was suffused with humanism, and in humanism Christianity and antiquity had a common criterion at their disposal. But while ancient apologetics was confronted with a humanism that was pagan in substance, the distinctive factor in modern apologetics is its confrontation with a humanism that is Christian in substance. I have discussed this problem in my essay, "Lessing und die Idee der Erziehung des Menschengeschlechts." [25] With this viewpoint in mind, I conducted lectures and discussions on apologetics in various private residences in Berlin. The results of these gatherings were summarized in a report to the governing body of the Evangelical Church; this action later led to the establishment of a commission for apologetics in home missions.

It was only after the war that the reality and nature of this Christian humanism were brought fully home to me. My contact with the Labor Movement, with the so-called dechristianized masses, showed me clearly that here too, within a humanistic framework, the Christian substance was hidden, even though this humanism looked like a materialistic philosophy that had long since been discredited by art and science. An apologetic message to the masses was even more necessary and more difficult than to the intelligentsia since the former's opposition to religion was heightened by class antagonism. The Church's attempt to frame an apologetic message without considering the class struggle was doomed to complete failure at the outset. Defending Christianity in this situation required active participation in the class struggle. Only religious socialism could carry the apologetic message to the proletarian masses. Religious socialism, not "inner mission," is the necessary form of Christian activity and apologetics among the working classes. The apologetic element in religious socialism has often been obscured by its political aspects so that the Church failed to understand the indirect importance of religious socialism for its work. It was understood much better by the socialists themselves, who often expressed to me their fear that religious socialism would bring the masses under the Church's influence and thus alienate them from the struggle to achieve a socialist government.

The Church also repudiated religious socialism because the movement either had to discard the traditional symbols and concepts of ecclesiastical thought and practice, or to use them only after a certain amount of groundwork had been laid. Had they been used indiscriminately, the proletariat would have automatically rejected them. The task of religious socialism was to demonstrate that implicit in the Christian humanism of the Labor Movement was the same substance as in the entirely different sacramental forms of the Church. A number of young theologians shared this understanding of Christian humanism; they accepted non-ecclesiastical positions, especially in the social services, for the express purpose of influencing religiously those whom no church official could have reached in any way. Unfortunately, such opportunities were available only to a few. And since the problems of "church and humanist society" and "church and proletariat" were of little significance to the younger theologians of the Barthian school, the chasm was never bridged by the Church. A disinte-

grated humanist society thus fell victim, in large meas-
ure, to neo-pagan tendencies. The Church was com-
pelled to fight these tendencies and thus to appear
even more anti-humanist. The proletariat sank back
into religious passivity. Though the intelligentsia came
to admire the Church for its stand against nationalistic
paganism, they were not drawn to it. The dogma de-
fended by the Church did not and could not appeal to
. them. In order to reach this group, the Church must
proclaim the gospel in a language that is comprehensi-
. ble to a non-ecclesiastical humanism. It would have to
convince both the intellectuals and the masses that the
gospel is of absolute relevance for them. But this conviction cannot be imparted by the pointedly anti-
humanist paradoxes that are used in confessional theology. The reality which gives rise to such paradoxes
must first be illuminated. But theologians like Brunner and Gogarten do not attempt the illumination.
They feed on humanism by negating it, for their
descriptions of the positive content of the Christian
proclamation consist of using and, at the same time,
negating that which they are opposing.

Grave problems arise whenever the question of the
language of the Christian gospel is taken seriously, as
it was by the *Neuwerkkreis* and in the magazine of

the same name which was edited by my old friend and comrade in this struggle, Hermann Schafft. It is certain that the original religious terminology of the Scriptures and the liturgies of the ancient Church cannot be supplanted. Mankind does have religious, archetypal words, as Martin Buber once remarked to me. But these archetypal words have been robbed of their original power by our objectifying way of thinking and by our scientific conception of the world. Rational criticism is powerless before the meaning of the archetypal word "God"; but atheism is a correct response to the "objectively" existing God of literalistic thought. A hopeless situation arises when a speaker uses a word in its original symbolic sense but the listener understands the word in a contemporary scientific sense. This is why I once proposed, for the sake of provocation, that the church impose a thirty-year moratorium on all of its archetypal language. Were this to happen, as it did in a few instances, the church would have to develop a new terminology. But attempts made thus far to translate the archaic language of liturgy and Scripture into contemporary idiom have been deplorable failures. They represent a depletion of meaning, not a new creation. Even using the terminology of the mystics, especially in sermons

—as I have sometimes done—is dangerous. A different content is conveyed by these words, a content that hardly covers all the substance of the Christian gospel. The only solution is to use the archetypal religious words while at the same time making their original meaning clear by disavowing their distorted usage. One must stand between the archaic and contemporary terminologies to recapture, on the boundary, the original archetypal language. The present peril of society has driven many to this boundary where the language of religion can be heard again in its original meaning. It would be regrettable if a blind and arrogant orthodoxy should monopolize these words and thus frighten away those who are sensitive to religious reality, either forcing them into some modern paganism or conclusively driving them out of the Church.

The problem of Church and Society prompted me, in an essay entitled "Kirche und humanistische Gesellschaft" (Church and Humanistic Society) [26], to draw a distinction between a "manifest" and a "latent" Church. This was not the old Protestant distinction between the visible and the invisible Church, but was concerned with a duality within the visible churches. The kind of distinction I suggested in that essay seems to be necessary in order to take into account the Christian humanism which exists outside the churches. It is not permissible to designate as "un-churched" those who have become alienated from organized denominations and traditional creeds. In living among these groups for half a generation I learned how much of the latent Church there is within them. I encountered the experience of the finite character of human existence, the quest for the eternal and uncon-ditioned, an absolute devotion to justice and love, a hope that lies beyond any Utopia, an appreciation of Christian values and a very sensitive recognition of the ideological misuse of Christianity in the interpenetra-tion of Church and State. It has often seemed to me that the "latent Church," as I call what I found among these groups, was a truer church than the organized denominations, if only because its members did not presume to possess the truth. The last few years have shown, however, that only the organized Church is capable of maintaining the struggle against the pagan attacks on Christianity. The latent Church has neither the religious nor the organizational weapons necessary for this struggle. But it is also true that the use of these weapons within the manifest Church threatens to deepen the chasm between Church and Society. The concept of the latent Church is a concept of the boundary on which countless Protestants in our day are fated to stand.

BETWEEN
RELIGION *AND* CULTURE

IF A PERSON who had been deeply moved by the mosaics of Ravenna, the ceiling paintings of the Sistine Chapel, or the portraits of the older Rembrandt, were asked whether his experience had been religious or cultural, he would find the question difficult to an-
. swer. It might be correct to say that the experience is
. cultural in form and religious in substance. It is cultural because it is not attached to a specific ritual act; but it is religious because it touches on the question of the Absolute and the limits of human existence. This is as true of music, poetry, philosophy and science as it is of painting. And whatever is true in this intuition and understanding of the world remains true in the practical work of shaping laws and customs, in morality
. and education, in community and state. Culture is religious wherever human existence is subjected to ulti-

mate questions and thus transcended; and wherever
unconditioned meaning becomes visible in works that
have only conditioned meaning in themselves. In ex-
periencing the substantially religious character of culture I came to the boundary between religion and culture, and I have never left it. My philosophy of
religion is chiefly concerned with the theoretical aspects of this boundary.

The relationship between religion and culture must
be defined from both sides of the boundary. Religion
cannot relinquish the absolute and, therefore, univer-
sal claim that is expressed in the idea of God. It cannot
allow itself to become a special area within culture, or
to take a position beside culture. Liberalism has tended
to interpret religion in one or the other of these ways.
In either case, religion becomes superfluous and must
disappear because the structure of culture is complete
and self-contained without religion. It is also true,
however, that culture has a claim on religion that it
cannot surrender without surrendering its autonomy
and therefore itself. It must determine the forms
through which every content, including the "absolute" content, expresses itself. Culture cannot allow
truth and justice to be sacrificed in the name of the
religious absolute. As religion is the substance of cul-

ture, so culture is the form of religion. Only one difference must be noted: religion's intentionality is toward substance, which is the unconditioned source and abyss of meaning, and cultural forms serve as symbols of that substance. Culture's intentionality is toward the form, representing conditioned meaning. The substance, representing unconditioned meaning, can be glimpsed only indirectly through the medium of the autonomous form granted by culture. Culture attains its highest expression where human existence is comprehended in its finitude and its quest for the Infinite within the framework of a complete, autonomous form. Conversely, religion in its highest expression must include the autonomous form, the Logos, as the ancient church called it, within itself.

These ideas constituted the basic principles of my philosophy of religion and culture and provided a framework for discussing the history of culture from a religious point of view. This explains why my book, *The Religious Situation*,[27] is concerned with the full range of intellectual and social movements in the immediate past, while religious questions, in the narrower sense, occupy less space. I have no doubt that this approach corresponds to the actual religious situation of the present. Political and social concerns have

absorbed the energies of religion to such a degree that
for great numbers of Europeans and Americans religious and political ideals coincide. The myths of the
nation and of social justice are widely replacing Christian doctrine and have had effects that can be re-
garded only as religious even though they appear in
cultural forms. The outline for a theological analysis
of culture that I developed in my lecture, "Über die
Idee einer Theologie der Kultur" (On the Idea of a
Theology of Culture) [28], takes into consideration the
course of recent history.

I sketched the theological consequences of these reflections in an article concerning the relation of Protestantism to Secularism. In it I argue that if Protestantism has any ruling passion it is toward the "profane." Such an idea rejects in principle the Catholic
separation of the sacred and the profane. In the presence of the Unconditioned (the Majesty of God, in
the traditional language of Christianity), there is no
preferred sphere. There are no persons, scriptures,
communities, institutions, or actions that are holy in
themselves, nor are there any that are profane in
themselves. The profane can profess the quality of
holiness, and the holy does not cease to be profane.
The priest is a layman, and the layman can become a

priest at any time. To me this is not only a theological principle, but also a position I have maintained professionally and personally. As a clergyman and theologian, I cannot be anything other than a layman and philosopher who has tried to say something about the limits of human existence. Nor have I any intention of concealing my theological endeavors. On the contrary, I have aired them where, for example, in my work as a professor of philosophy, they could easily have been concealed. But I did not want to develop a theological habitude that would set me apart from profane life and earn me the label "religious." It seems to me that the unconditioned character of religion becomes far more manifest if it breaks out from within the secular, disrupting and transforming it. I likewise believe that the dynamic dimension of the religious is betrayed when certain institutions and personalities are considered to be religious in themselves. To think of the clergyman as a man whose faith is a professional requirement borders on blasphemy.

My response to efforts at reforming the ritual of the German church stems from this conviction. I joined the so-called *Berneuchen* movement which was led by Wilhelm Stählin and Karl Ritter. This group urged more rigorous reforms than all other reforming

Secular christianity

groups, and it did not limit itself to matters of ritual. These men sought first of all to formulate a clearly defined theological basis for reform. Thus I had an opportunity for fruitful theological collaboration. Ritual acts, forms and attitudes do not contradict a "passion for the secular" if they are understood for what they are: symbolic forms in which the religious substance that supports our entire existence is represented in a unique way. The meaning of a ritual or sacramental act is not that the act is holy in itself, but that it is a symbol of the Unconditioned which alone is holy and which is, and is not, in all things at the same time.

In a lecture entitled "Natur und Sakrament" (Nature and Sacrament) [29], delivered at a conference of the Berneuchen group, I tried to explain the distinction between the non-sacramental, intellectualistic thinking of Protestantism and humanism and the original meaning of sacramental thinking, which was lost in the late medieval period. Within the framework of Protestantism, this is a difficult but necessary task. No church is possible without a sacramental representation of the holy. It was this conviction that bound me to the Berneuchen group. However, I could not go along with them when they moved away from our

mutual concern with the boundary between the secular and the sacred, to an exclusive preoccupation with
(often archaic) liturgical forms. Here again, I am
convinced that I must stay on the boundary.

BETWEEN
LUTHERANISM AND
SOCIALISM

IT IS comparatively easy to move into socialism from
Calvinism, especially in the more secularized forms of
later Calvinism. By way of Lutheranism, the road to
socialism is very difficult. I am a Lutheran by birth,
education, religious experience, and theological reflection. I have never stood on the boundary between
Lutheranism and Calvinism, not even after I experienced the disastrous consequences of Lutheran social
ethics and came to recognize the inestimable value of
the Calvinistic idea of the Kingdom of God in the
solution of social problems. The substance of my reli-

74

gion is and remains Lutheran. It includes a consciousness of the "corruption" of existence, a repudiation of
every kind of social Utopia (including the metaphysics of progressivism), an awareness of the irrational
and demonic nature of existence, an appreciation of
the mystical element in religion, and a rejection of
Puritanical legalism in private and corporal life. My
philosophical thinking also expresses this unique content. Up to now, only Jacob Boehme, the philosophical spokesman for German mysticism, has attempted a
specifically philosophical elaboration of Lutheranism.
Through Boehme, Lutheran mysticism influenced
Schelling and German idealism, and through Schelling
it in turn influenced the philosophies of irrationalism
and vitalism that emerged in the nineteenth and twen-
tieth centuries. To the extent that much anti-socialist
ideology has been based on irrationalism and vitalism,
Lutheranism has worked indirectly through philosophy, as well as directly, to check socialism.

The course of German theology after the war
shows very clearly that it is practically impossible for
a people educated as Lutherans to move from religion
to socialism. Two theological movements, both Lutheran, were opposed to religious socialism. The first
was the religious nationalism which called itself

"young Lutheran" theology; its chief proponent was
Emmanuel Hirsch, a one-time fellow student and
friend who was to become my theological and political opponent. The second was Barthian theology,
which is wrongly called "dialectical theology." Although Barth's theology has many Calvinistic elements, his strongly transcendent idea of the Kingdom
of God is definitely Lutheran. Both Barthian theology's indifference to social questions and Hirsch's
sanctification of nationalism are so consistent with
religious, social, and political traditions in Germany
that it was futile for religious socialism to oppose
them. But the fact that religious socialism had no future on German soil did not imply that it was theolog-
ically wrong or politically unnecessary. The impossibility of uniting religion and socialism will be recognized in the near or distant future as a tragic element
in German history.

Standing on the boundary between Lutheranism
and religious socialism requires first of all a critical
confrontation with the problem of Utopianism. The
Lutheran doctrine of man, even in the naturalistic
form it takes in vitalism, negates all Utopianism. Sin,
cupidity, the will to power, the unconscious urge, or
any other word used to describe the human situation

is so bound up with the existence of man and nature (not, of course, with their essence or creaturely endowment) that establishing the Kingdom of justice and peace within the realm of estranged reality is impossible. The Kingdom of God can never be fulfilled in time and space. Every Utopianism is doomed to metaphysical disappointment. However changeable human nature may be, it is not amenable to fundamental moral correction. Improvements in education and environment may serve to raise the general ethical level of a people and to polish its original crudeness, but such improvements do not affect the freedom to do good and evil as long as man is man. Mankind does not become better; good and evil are merely raised to a higher plane.

With these considerations, which are drawn directly from the Lutheran understanding of human existence, I have touched on a problem which has become more and more important to socialist thinking and which is of particular concern to religious socialism—the problem of the doctrine of man. I am convinced that a false anthropology has robbed religious socialism of its persuasive force, particularly in Germany. A politician who does not admit the truth about man (in Luther's phrase, "what there is in man") cannot be successful. On the other hand, I do not believe that the Lutheran conception, especially in its naturalistic versions, i.e., in vitalism and fascism, has the last word to say about man. The prophetic message may point the way here as elsewhere. The prophetic message is that human nature shall be transformed together with all nature. Even though this belief implies a miracle, it is more realistic than those views which leave nature unchanged while striving to transform man. They represent Utopianism, not the paradox of prophetic expectation.

Long before the anthropological implications of Utopianism were clearly understood, the utopian problem was the central issue in the religious socialist movement. We met shortly after the Russian Revolution of 1917 to discuss religion and socialism. In these first meetings, it became clear that our basic issue was the relationship of religion to some kind of social Utopianism. It was then that I first used the New Testament concept of the Kairos, the fullness of time, which as a boundary concept between religion and socialism has been the hallmark of German religious socialism. The concept of the fullness of time indicates that the struggle for a new social order cannot lead to the kind of fulfillment expressed by the idea of the

Kingdom of God, but that at a particular time particular tasks are demanded, as one particular aspect of
the Kingdom of God becomes a demand and an expectation for us. The Kingdom of God will always ·
remain transcendent, but it appears as a judgment on a
given form of society and as a norm for a coming one.
Thus, the decision to be a religious socialist may be a
decision for the Kingdom of God even though the
socialist society is infinitely distant from the Kingdom
of God. I edited and contributed to two volumes,
Kairos: Vol. 1. *Zur Geisteslage und Geisteswendung* [30]
and Vol. 2. *Protestantismus als Kritik und Gestaltung,*[31]
in which the idea of the Kairos is explored in its theological and philosophical presuppositions and implications.

A very important concept related to the "Kairos"
idea is that of the demonic. I have discussed it in the
essay "On the Demonic." [32] This concept could not
have been developed without the groundwork laid by
Lutheran mysticism and philosophical irrationalism.
The demonic is a power in personal and social life that ·
is creative and destructive at the same time. In the ·
New Testament, men possessed by demons are said to
know more about Jesus than those who are normal,
but they know it as a condemnation of themselves be-

cause they are divided against themselves. The early
church called the Roman Empire demonic because it
made itself equal to God, and yet the church prayed
for the emperor and gave thanks for the civic peace he
assured. Similarly, religious socialism tries to show
that capitalism and nationalism are demonic powers,
insofar as they are simultaneously destructive and
creative, and attribute divinity to their system of values. The course of European nationalism and Russian
communism and their quasi-religious self-justification
has fully confirmed this diagnosis.

It is not surprising that my earlier ideas regarding
the relations between religion and culture, the sacred
and the secular, heteronomy and autonomy, were in-
corporated into my reflections on religious socialism,
which thus became the focal point for all my thinking. Above all, socialism provided a theoretical foundation and practical impetus as I attempted to evolve a
theonomous philosophy of history. By analyzing the
character of "historical" time, as distinguished from
physical and biological time, I developed a concept of
history in which the movement toward the new,
which is both demanded and expected, is constitutive.
The content of the new, toward which history moves,
appears in events in which the meaning and goal of

history become manifest. I called such an event the "center of history"; from the Christian viewpoint the center is the appearance of Jesus as the Christ. The powers struggling with one another in history can be given different names, according to the perspective from which they are viewed: demonic-*divine*-human, sacramental-*prophetic*-secular, heteronomous-*theonomous*-autonomous. Each middle term represents the synthesis of the other two, the one toward which history is always extending itself—sometimes creatively, sometimes destructively, never completely fulfilled, but always driven by the transcendent power of the anticipated fulfillment. Religious socialism should be understood as one such move toward a new theonomy. It is more than a new economic system. It is a comprehensive understanding of existence, the form of the theonomy demanded and expected by our present Kairos.

BETWEEN

IDEALISM AND MARXISM

I GREW UP in the atmosphere of German idealism, and doubt that I can ever forget what I learned from it.

Above all I am indebted to Kant's critique of knowledge, which showed me that the question of the possibility of empirical knowledge cannot be answered
✳ merely by pointing to the realm of objects. _Every
analysis of experience and every systematic interpretation of reality must begin at the point where subject
. and object meet._ It is in this sense that I understand
the idealist principle of identity. It is not an example
of metaphysical speculation, but a principle for analyzing the basic character of all knowledge. To date
no critique of _idealism_ has convinced me that this
procedure is incorrect. By taking this principle as my
point of departure, I have been able to avoid all forms
. of metaphysical and naturalistic positivism. Thus I am
_epistemologically an idealist, if idealism means the
assertion of the identity of thought and being as the
. principle of truth._ Furthermore, it seems to me that
the element of freedom is given expression in the
idealistic conception of the world in a way that best
corresponds to subjective and objective experience.
The fact that man asks questions, his recognition of
absolute demands (the categorical imperative) in
thought and action, his perception of meaningful
forms in nature, art, and society (as in modern *Gestalt*
theories)—all these have convinced me that a doctrine

of man must be a philosophy of freedom. Nor can I deny that there is a correspondence between reality and the human spirit which is probably expressed most adequately in the concept of "meaning." It led Hegel to speak of the unity of objective and subjective spirit in an Absolute Spirit. When idealism elaborates the categories that give meaning to the various realms of existence, it seeks to fulfill that task which alone is the justification for philosophy.

It was an altogether different issue that led me to the boundary of idealism. The idealists claim that their system of categories portrays reality as a whole, rather than being the expression of a definite and existentially limited encounter with reality. Only Schelling in his second period was conscious of the limitation of idealistic or essentialist systems. He recognized that reality is not only the manifestation of pure essence but also its contradiction and, above all, that human existence itself is an expression of the contradiction of essence. Schelling realized that thought is also bound to existence and shares its contradiction of essence (which does not necessarily imply that it is defective). Schelling did not develop this seminal idea. Like Hegel, he believed that he and his philosophy stood at the end of a historical process through which the contradictions within existence had been overcome and an absolute standpoint attained. Schelling's idealism triumphed over his initial efforts at existential thinking. ι—Kierkegaard was the first to break through the closed system of the idealist philosophy of essence. His radical interpretation of the anxiety and despair of life led to a philosophy that could really be called existentialist. The importance of his work for post-war German theology and philosophy can hardly be overestimated. As early as in my last student years (1905–1906), I came under the influence of his aggressive dialectics.

During this same period, opposition to the idealist philosophy of being flared up from another direction. Hegel's radical followers, who came out against their teacher and "turned idealism on its head," proclaimed a theoretical and practical materialism in idealist categories. Karl Marx, who was a member of this group, went even further. He rejected both the idealist categories and their materialistic inversion (cf. his *Theses against Feuerbach*), and advocated a position that was directed against philosophy as such. This new position was "not to explain, but to change the world." According to Marx, philosophy—which he identified with the philosophy of essence—seeks to obscure the contradictions within existence, to abstract from that which is really important to human beings, namely the social contradictions that determine their lives in the world. These contradictions, or more specifically the conflict of the social classes, show that idealism is an ideology, that is, a system of concepts whose function is to veil the ambiguities of reality. (Analogously, Kierkegaard showed that the philosophy of essence tended to conceal the ambiguities within individual existence.)

First and foremost I owe to Marx an insight into the ideological character not only of idealism but also of all systems of thought, religious and secular, which serve power structures and thus prevent, even if unconsciously, a more just organization of reality. Luther's warning against the self-made God is the religious equivalent of what ideology means for philosophy.

A new definition of truth follows from the repudiation of the closed system of essentialism. Truth is bound to the situation of the knower: to the situation of the individual for Kierkegaard, and to that of society for Marx. Knowledge of pure essence is possible only to the degree in which the contradictions within existence have been recognized and overcome. In the situation of despair (the condition of every human being according to Kierkegaard), and in the situation of class struggle (the historical condition of humanity according to Marx), every closed and harmonious system is untrue. Both Kierkegaard and Marx, therefore, seek to associate truth with a particular psychological or social situation. For Kierkegaard truth is subjectivity which does not deny its despair and its exclusion from the world of essence, but which passionately affirms truth within this condition. For Marx, the locus of truth is the class-interest of the class that becomes aware of its destiny to overcome class conflict, that is, the non-ideological class. In both instances we learn, amazingly—though understandably from the Christian standpoint—that the highest possibility for achieving non-ideological truth is given at the point of profoundest meaninglessness, through the deepest despair, in man's greatest estrangement from his own nature. In an essay entitled *Das Protestantische Prinzip und die proletarische Situation* (The Protestant Principle and the Proletarian Situation) [33], I have related this idea to the Protestant principle and its doctrine concerning the human boundary situation. Of course, this is possible only if the notion of proletariat is used typologically. The actual proletariat at times corresponds to the proletarian type even less than some of the non-proletarian groups do —such as, for example, those intellectuals who have broken through their class situation to a boundary situation from which they are able to bring the proletariat to self-consciousness. One should not identify the proletarian masses with the typological concept of the proletariat as used by Marx.

Commonly understood, the word Marxism implies "economic materialism." But, intentionally or not, this combination of words overlooks the ambiguity in the term materialism. If materialism could mean only "metaphysical materialism," I should never have found myself on the boundary of Marxism, and Marx himself, who struggled against both materialism and idealism, would have been no Marxist. We should remember that economic materialism is not a metaphysics but a method of historical analysis. It does not imply that the "economic," which itself is a complex factor relating to all sides of human existence, is the sole principle for interpreting history. That would be a meaningless assertion. Economic materialism, however, does show the fundamental significance of economic structures and motives for the social and intellectual forms and changes in a historical period. It denies that there can be a history of thought and religion independent of economic factors, and thereby confirms the theological insight, neglected by idealism, that man lives on earth and not in heaven (or, in philosophical terms, that man lives within existence and not in the realm of essence).

Marxism can be understood as a method for unmasking hidden levels of reality. As such, it can be compared with psychoanalysis. Unmasking is painful and, in certain circumstances, destructive. Ancient Greek tragedy, e.g., the Oedipus myth, shows this clearly. Man defends himself against the revelation of his actual nature for as long as possible. Like Oedipus, he collapses when he sees himself without the ideologies that sweeten his life and prop up his self-consciousness. The passionate rejection of Marxism and pychoanalysis, which I have frequently encountered, is an attempt made by individuals and groups to escape an unmasking that can conceivably destroy them. But without this painful process the ultimate meaning of the Christian gospel cannot be perceived. The theologian, therefore, should use these means for exposing the true condition of man as often as he can rather than propagating an idealism that smoothes over the ambiguities of existence. He can do so from his position on the boundary—he can, as I have tried to do myself, criticize the partially obsolete terminology of psychoanalysis; he can reject the utopian and dogmatic elements in Marxism; and he can dispense with the many individual theories of both psychoanalysis and Marxism that lack scientific validity. The theologian can and must resist metaphysical and ethical materialism, whether or not it is a legitimate interpretation of Freud or Marx. But he must not deprive himself of either movement's efficacy in shattering ideologies and revealing the realities of human existence.

But Marxism has not only an "unmasking" effect; it involves also demand and expectation, and, as such, it has had and continues to have a tremendous impact on history. There is prophetic passion in it, whereas idealism, insofar as it has been molded by the principle of identity, has mystical and sacramental roots. In the central section of my book *Die socialistische Entscheidung* (Socialist Decision) [34], I tried to distinguish the prophetic elements in Marxism from its rational-scientific terminology and thus to make more comprehensible its far-reaching religious and historical implications. I also tried to gain a new understanding of the socialist principle by comparing it with the tenets of

Judeo-Christian prophecy. Marxists may accuse me of idealism and idealists may complain of my materialism, but I am actually on the boundary between the two. Marxism has become a slogan for defaming political opponents. Admitting that I stand on the boundary of Marxism adds nothing new politically to what I have said about my relationship to religious socialism. It does not commit me to any political party. Were I to say that I have stood between two political parties, the "between" would have to be interpreted differently than it has been elsewhere in these pages. It would mean that I do not inwardly belong to any party and never have, because what seems to me most important in the political realm is something that is never fully manifest in political parties. I desire and always have desired a fellowship that is bound to no party, although it may be nearer to one than to another. This group should be the vanguard for a more righteous social order, established in the prophetic spirit and in accord with the demand of the Kairos.

BETWEEN
NATIVE AND ALIEN LAND

MY WRITING this self-portrait in an alien country is a destiny that, like all true destiny, represents freedom at the same time. The boundary between native land and alien country is not merely an external boundary marked off by nature or by history. It is also the boundary between two inner forces, two possibilities of human existence, whose classic formulation is the command to Abraham: "Go from your home . . . to the land that I will show you." He is bidden to leave his native soil, the community of his family and cult, his people and state, for the sake of a promise that he does not understand. The God who demands obedience of him is the God of an alien country, a God not bound to the local soil, as are pagan deities, but the God of history, who means to bless all the races of the earth. This God, the God of the prophet and of Jesus, utterly demolishes all religious nationalism—the nationalism of the Jews, which he opposes constantly, and that of the pagans, which is repudiated in the command to Abraham. For the Christian of any confession, the meaning of this command is indisputable. He must ever leave his own country and enter into a land that will be shown to him. He must trust a promise that is purely transcendent.

The real meaning of "homeland" varies according to the situation of the individual. It may be the land of his birth and his national community. Occasionally, "physical emigration" may be demanded. But the command to go from one's country is more often a call to break with ruling authorities and prevailing social and political patterns, and to resist them passively or actively. It is a demand for "spiritual emigration" —the Christian community's attitude toward the Roman Empire. The path into an alien country may also signify something wholly personal and inward: parting from accepted lines of belief and thought; pushing beyond the limits of the obvious; radical questioning that opens up the new and uncharted. In Nietzsche's words, it means moving into "the land of our children" and out of "the land of our fathers and mothers." It is a temporal, not a geographical, emigration. The alien land lies in the future, the country "beyond the present." And when we speak of this alien country we also point to our recognition that even what is nearest and most familiar to us contains an element of strangeness. This is the metaphysical experience of being alone in the world that existentialism takes as its expression of human finitude.

In every sense of the word, I have always stood between native and alien land. I have never decided exclusively for the alien, and I have experienced both types of "emigration." I began to be an "emigrant" personally and spiritually long before I actually left my homeland.

My attachment to my native land in terms of landscape, language, tradition and mutuality of historical destiny has always been so instinctive that I could never understand why it should have to be made an object of special attention. The overemphasis of cultural nationalism in national education and intellectual productivity is an expression of insecurity about national ties. I am convinced that this overemphasis occurs in individuals who come from the boundary—either externally or internally—and who feel obligated, therefore, to justify their patriotism to themselves and to others. They are also afraid to return to the boundary.

I have always felt so thoroughly German by nature that I could not dwell on the fact at length. Conditions of birth and destiny cannot really be questioned. We should instead ask: What shall we do with this which is given in our lives? What should be our criterion for evaluating society and politics, intellectual and moral training, cultural and social life? Accidents of birth do not constitute answers to such questions, because the questions presuppose them. If the presuppositions are mistaken for the answers we find ourselves caught in the vicious circle that today is praised as national feeling, although it testifies to a lack of confidence in the strength of our national substance and leads to a terrible emptiness of national life. I expressed my opposition to such nationalistic tendencies in my Frankfurt lectures on public education: "Sozialpädagogik" (Social Education).

Today, however, the problem of nationalism is primarily an economic and political problem. I have held varying attitudes toward it. In an article on the totalitarian state and the claims of the church, I discussed the causes of militant totalitarianism in Europe and its relationship to the disintegration of capitalism. My essay, "Das Problem der Macht" (On the Philosophy of Power) [35], deals with the meaning and limits of power as it is related to the general problem of Being, that is, ontology. In *Die socialistische Entscheidung*,[36]

I tried to lay bare the anthropological roots and political consequences of nationalism. The experience of World War I was crucial for my position. It revealed the demonic and destructive character of the national will to power, particularly for those who went to war enthusiastically and with a firm belief in the justice of their national cause. Consequently, I can only view European nationalism as an instrument for the tragic self-destruction of Europe even though—or perhaps because—I realize that nationalism is inevitable. But this insight never made me a pacifist, in the strict sense of the word. One type of pacifism is suspect to me because of the effeminate character of its representatives. The kind of pacifism advocated by victorious and self-satisfied nations has an ideological and pharisaic taint. For such nations pacifism is too useful to be honest. Legalistic pacifism, in my opinion, ends in consequences which are opposite from those intended. In this world, national as well as international peace depends on the power to restrain the violators of peace. I am not speaking in justification of a national will to power; but I recognize the necessity for interconnected forces, behind which there must be a power capable of preventing the self-destruction of mankind. Today the idea of "mankind" is more than an empty notion. It has become an economic and political reality; for the fate of every part of the world depends on the fate of every other part. The increasing realization of a united mankind represents and anticipates, so to speak, the truth implicit in a belief in the Kingdom of God to which all nations and all races belong. Denying the unity of mankind as aim includes, therefore, denying the Christian doctrine that the Kingdom of God is "at hand." I was happy to discover on the boundary of this new continent where I now live, thanks to American hospitality, an ideal which is more consistent with the image of one mankind than that of Europe in her tragic self-dismemberment. It is the image of one nation in whom representatives of all nations and races can live as citizens. Although here too the distance between ideal and reality is infinite and the image is often deeply shadowed, nonetheless it is a kind of symbol of that highest possibility of history which is called "mankind," and which itself points to that which transcends reality— the Kingdom of God. In that highest possibility, the boundary between native and alien land ceases to exist.

RETROSPECT:
BOUNDARY AND
LIMITATION

MANY POSSIBILITIES of human existence, both physical
and spiritual, have been discussed in these pages. Some
things have not been mentioned, although they are
part of my biography. Many more things have been
left untouched, because they do not belong to the
story of my life and thought. Each possibility that I
have discussed, however, I have discussed in its relationship to another possibility—the way they are
opposed, the way they can be correlated. This is the
dialectic of existence; each of life's possibilities drives
of its own accord to a boundary and beyond the
boundary where it meets that which limits it. The
man who stands on many boundaries experiences the
unrest, insecurity, and inner limitation of existence in
many forms. He knows the impossibility of attaining
serenity, security, and perfection. This holds true in

life as well as in thought, and may explain why the experiences and ideas which I have recounted are rather
fragmentary and tentative. My desire to give definitive form to these thoughts has once again been frus-
trated by my boundary-fate, which has cast me on the
soil of a new continent. Completing such a task to the
best of my ability is a hope that becomes more uncer-
tain as I approach fifty. But whether or not it is to be
fulfilled, there remains a boundary for human activity
which is no longer a boundary between two possibilities but rather a limit set on everything finite by that
which transcends all human possibilities, the Eternal.
In its presence, even the very center of our being is
only a boundary and our highest level of accomplish-
ment is fragmentary.

NOTES

1. Religiöse Verwirklichung. Berlin: Furche, 1929.

2. "Logos und Mythos der Technik." Logos (Tübingen), XVI, No. 3 (November, 1927).

3. "Die technische Stadt als Symbol." Dresdner Neueste Nachrichten, No. 115 (May 17, 1928).

4. The Religious Situation. New York: Henry Holt, 1932.

5. "Masse und Geist." Studien zur Philosophie der Masse. "Volk und Geist," No. 1 Berlin/Frankfurt a.M.: Verlag der Arbeitsgemeinschaft, 1922.

6. "Grundlinien des religiösen Sozialismus. Ein systematischer Entwurf." Blätter fur Religiösen Sozialismus (Berlin), IV, No. 8/10 (1923).

7. Die sozialistische Entscheidung. Potsdam: Alfred Protte, 1933.

8. "Das Problem der Macht. Versuch einer philosophischen Grundlegung." Neue Blätter fur den Sozialismus (Potsdam), II, No. 4 (April, 1931).

9. Das System der Wissenschaften nach Gegenständen und Methoden. Ein Entwurf. Göttingen: Vandenhoeck & Ruprecht, 1923.

10. Die sozialistische Entscheidung. Potsdam: Alfred Protte, 1933.

11. The Religious Situation. New York: Henry Holt, 1932.

12. "Masse und Persönlichkeit." Göttingen: Vandenhoeck & Ruprecht, 1920.

13. Das System der Wissenschaften nach Gegenständen und Methoden. Ein Entwurf. Göttingen: Vandenhoeck & Ruprecht, 1923.

14. "Religionsphilosophie." Lehrbuch der Philosophie, ed. Max Dessoir. Vol. II: Die Philosophie in ihren Einzelgebieten. Berlin: Ullstein, 1925.

15. Neue Blätter für den Sozialismus. Potsdam: Alfred Protte, 1931.

16. Protestantismus als Kritik und Gestaltung. Darmstadt: Otto Reichl, 1929.

17. Religiöse Verwirklichung. Berlin: Furche, 1929.

18. "Der Staat als Erwartung und Forderung." In: Religiöse Verwirklichung. Berlin: Furche, 1929.

19. "The Totalitarian State and the Claims of the Church." Social Research (New York) 1, No. 4 (November, 1934).

20. Masse und Geist. Studien zur Philosophie der Masse. Berlin/Frankfurt a.M.: Verlag der Arbeitsgemeinschaft, 1922.

21. "Rechtfertigung und Zweifel." Vorträge der theologischen Konferenz zu Giessen, 39. Folge, Giessen: Alfred Töpelmann, 1924.

22. "Die Idee der Offenbarung." Zeitschrift fur Theologie und Kirche (Tübingen), N.F., VIII, No. 6 (1927).

23. "Die Überwindung des Religionsbegriffs in der Religionsphilosophie." Kant-Studien (Berlin), XXVII, No. 3/4 (1922).

24. Das System der Wissenschaften nach Gegenständen und Methoden. Ein Entwurf. Göttingen. Vandenhoeck & Ruprecht, 1923.

25. Religiöse Verwirklichung. Berlin: Furche, 1929.

26. "Kirche und humanistische Gesellschaft." Neuwerk (Kassel), XIII, No. 1 (April–May, 1931).

27. The Religious Situation. New York: Henry Holt, 1932.

28. "Über die Idee einer Theologie der Kultur." Religionsphilosophie der Kultur. Berlin: Reuther & Reichard, 1919.

29. "Natur und Sakrament." In: Religiöse Verwirklichung. Berlin: Furche, 1929.

30. Kairos: Zur Geisteslage und Geisteswendung. Darmstadt: Otto Reichl, 1926.

31. Protestantismus als Kritik und Gestaltung. Darmstadt: Otto Reichl, 1929.

32. The Interpretation of History. New York: Scribners, 1936.

33. Protestantisches Prinzip und proletarische Situation: Bonn: F. Cohen, 1931.

34. Die sozialistische Entscheidung. Potsdam: Alfred Protte, 1933.

35. "Das Problem der Macht. Versuch einer philosophischen Grundlegung." Neue Blätter für den Sozialismus (Potsdam), II, No. 4 (April, 1931).

36. Die sozialistische Entscheidung. Potsdam: Alfred Protte, 1933.